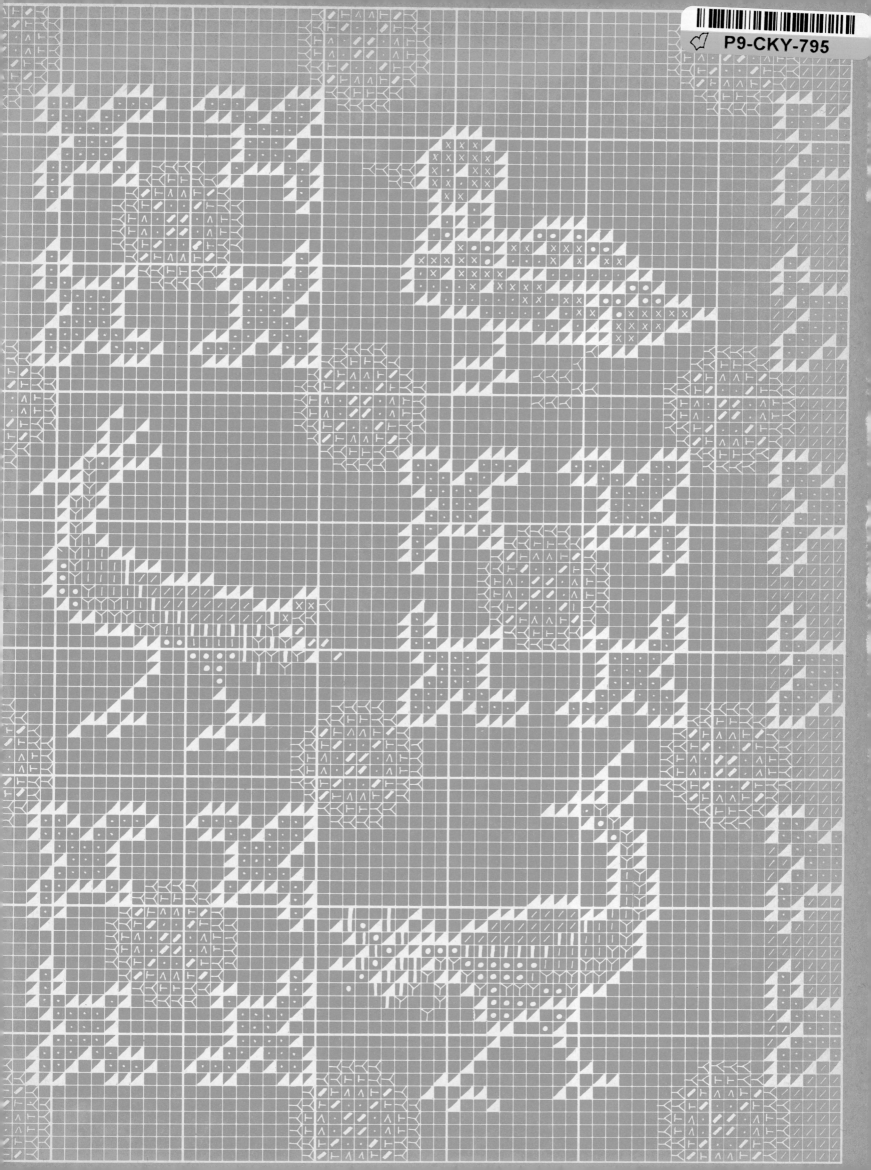
P9-CKY-795

*Needlepoint Designs from the Mosaics of Ravenna*

*Ann Roth*

# Needlepoint Designs from the Mosaics of Ravenna

Charles Scribner's Sons · New York

Color photographs, Judy and Kenny, Tel Aviv
Black and white photographs, Photo Alinari, Florence

The interior appearing on pp. 32–33 was photographed
at Eurodesign, Interior Architects, Ramat Hasharon, Israel.

Designed by Zvi Narkiss

Copyright © 1975 Massada Press, Jerusalem

Copyright under the Berne Convention

All rights reserved. No part of this book may be
reproduced in any form without the permission of
Charles Scribner's Sons.

Printed in Israel
Library of Congress Catalog Card Number 75–4401
ISBN 0–684–14469–7

# CONTENTS

Ravenna, now a silent and solitary city, has had a great past, part of which is documented by the many richly decorated monuments which have survived. Only a few fragments — inscriptions, sarcophagi, and marble ornaments — shed light on Ravenna's Roman glory from the time of Augustus Caesar. The emperor made Classe, the great seaport of Ravenna, the base of his Adriatic fleet. At the beginning of the fifth century Honorius, ruler of the western part of the late Roman Empire, settled in Ravenna while subsequently, from 425 to 450, his sister Galla Placidia governed as regent for her son Valentinian III and gave the city the appearance of a royal capital. Theodoric the Goth, king of Italy from 493 to 526, made Ravenna his residence and continued to adorn it with monuments. Finally Justinian (527–565), the Byzantine emperor who reconquered Italy, took Ravenna as his capital and made it the seat of Byzantine government in the West. After Justinian the fortunes of the city gradually declined. But the two centuries of its zenith are marked by a large number of structures, in many of which a magnificent series of mosaics is preserved, making Ravenna the richest repository in the western world of Early Christian and Byzantine mosaics.

The earliest preserved monument is the "Mausoleum of Galla Placidia," a small vaulted edifice built in the mid-fifth century and decorated with gorgeous mosaics. The symbols of the Evangelists, the Apostles, the Good Shepherd, and St. Lawrence hurrying to the fire of martyrdom, deer, doves, fruits, flowers, leaves, crosses, and similar decorative items are set in the deep azure background of its walls and its roof which is aglow with golden stars.

Between the death of Placidia and the advent of Theodoric the orthodox Baptistery of S. Piero Maggiore was erected and decorated. This structure is in the shape of a domed octagon and is covered from top to bottom with mosaics and stuccoes originally in color. The motifs are again the Apostles and prophets, but altars and thrones supporting crosses also appear. At the center of the dome the Baptism of Christ is represented.

Only a few of Theodoric's superb edifices have remained. A chapel dedicated to St. Andrew was built inside the Archbishop's palace and adorned with magnificent mosaics. On the cupola appear the four Evangelists with their symbols and on the vaults, a series of heads including those of Christ and the Apostles. The margins of the walls bear colored stylized decoration.

# The Mosaic Art of Ravenna: An Introduction

The greatest and one of the most beautiful of Theodoric's basilicas is that known today as Sant' Apollinare Nuovo, which was originally built as his mausoleum. It is decorated with wonderful mosaics potraying on one side the miracles of Christ and on the other the episodes of the Passion. Some of Theodoric's mosaics were replaced in Justinian's time by a long procession of martyrs on one side and of virgins on the other, marching toward the apse to offer their crowns to Christ and to the Virgin.

Theodoric, who was an adherent of the Arian faith, built the Baptistery of the Arians, also decorated with mosaics. On the cupola are depicted the twelve Apostles holding crowns, and at the center of the dome, the Baptism of Christ.

During the time of Justinian Ravenna greatly increased in wealth and splendor under imperial patronage. To this period belongs the completion of two edifices celebrated for their significance and grandeur.

The Church of San Vitale, "beautiful as an oriental dream" and "purest glory of Byzantine art in the West," was completed in 547. If its mosaics no longer breathe the classical sentiment of the earlier ones, they surpass all others in wealth of design and richness of color, as well as in artistic, historical, and symbolical interest. On the walls of the presbytery and apse are scenes from the Old Testament — the sacrifices of Abel, Melchizedek and Abraham — encompassing prophets, the Apostles and saints, the Evangelists with their symbols, and Christ, demonstrating the harmony of the Old Testament with the New. The vaults of San Vitale are adorned with ornaments: flowers, fruits, beasts, and angels.

The brilliant light, the freshness of the colors, and the blaze of gold are intensified under the vault of the apse, which seems to burst into flames behind the altar of precious alabaster and over the rich intaglia of marble. Justinian, clad in purple and crowned with the imperial diadem, accompanied by his assistants and the bishop, offers gold in a large basin for the construction of the basilica. The empress Theodora, crowned with the precious Byzantine diadem aglow with gems, and the ladies of her court look down from the opposite wall.

The embroidered garments, the jewels, the ornamented frames, the dressing of the hair are all portrayed with extreme care, as if to give to the west a true picture of the magnificence of the Byzantine court.

The other monument erected in this period, Sant' Apollinare in Classe, was built on the model of the Roman basilica. The magnificence of this edifice stems from its wonderful marble columns and its architectural perfection. The mosaic decoration is confined to the vault of the apse, showing Christ between the symbols of the Evangelists and lambs marching from two cities. Other mosaics, sparsely distributed between the windows, are of later date and inferior quality.

Ravenna holds a supreme place in the history of art. Since secular monuments of the period with their wall paintings and mosaics have not survived, its churches are a source of our knowledge of Byzantine decorative arts. We know, for instance, that little attention was paid to the exterior, while the interiors were most richly and imaginatively adorned. Usually, the lower part of the walls was decorated with colored marble panels, while mosaics were affixed on the upper parts, close to the windows that gave them proper lighting. Mosaics also covered the dome, apses, and vaults.

The Early Church rejected the representation of sacred themes and images. Early Christian art, therefore, borrowed pagan motifs and endowed them with symbolic Christian meaning. Scenes of vintage represented the salvation of the soul, doves became the symbol of future life, and the good shepherd or the lamb, symbols of Christ. This early tradition is clearly seen in the Mausoleum of Galla Placidia — the stags at the fountain of life and doves drinking from springs — as well as in the Baptistery where the main decorative motif of the lower vaults are garlands among whose branches appear small figures of the Apostles, representing eternal bliss in Paradise.

Later this tradition was changed in Syria and Palestine, where the definitive character of Christian iconography was formed. The symbolic pagan motifs were abandoned, and a trend to realistic representation of scenes from the Old and New Testaments developed. It is this new trend which receives its full expression in Ravenna, in the earlier buildings along with the old tradition, culminating in the twenty-six scenes from the Passion in Sant' Apollinare Nuovo and in the Old and New Testament scenes in San Vitale. Nowhere else can both traditions of Byzantine art be found side by side in such perfect expression as in the mosaics of "Felix Ravenna."

JUDITH SPITZER

# *Doves at the Fountain*

SO-CALLED MAUSOLEUM OF GALLA PLACIDIA

Galla Placidia, daughter of Emperor Theodosius, reigned over the West Roman Empire as regent for her minor son.

The cruciform chapel was part of the church of Santa Croce during the reign of Galla Placidia. She intended the chapel to be her future mausoleum, but as she died in Rome (450) it is doubtful whether she was buried here. The chapel is a simple brick building, consisting of a square tower and four cross-arms. Blind arcades give rhythm and variety to the wall surface.

*DOVES AT THE FOUNTAIN* (DETAIL, CROSS-ARM). *The Apostles, dressed in white priests' vestments, are depicted on either side of the translucent alabaster windows. At their feet white doves drink from fountains, symbolizing the good Christian and everlasting life.*

# Star-Studded Background

SO-CALLED MAUSOLEUM OF GALLA PLACIDIA

Inside the chapel nothing is seen of the remarkable angularity which characterizes the exterior. All the lines flow together, creating a colorful and harmonious impression. Salvation is the principal theme, shown by the picture of the Good Shepherd, the martyrdom of St. Lawrence, and many Christian symbols. The dome is totally covered with mosaics. A golden cross is placed in a deep blue sky, studded with stars; around it are the symbols of the four Evangelists.

The vault of the arms is decorated with ornamental motifs on a deep blue background.

*STAR-STUDDED BACKGROUND* (VAULT OF THE ARMS). *This mosaic pattern resembles an oriental carpet. Although the artists are unknown, it is very likely that they took their inspiration from oriental art.*

# Stags at the Fountain of Life

SO-CALLED MAUSOLEUM OF GALLA PLACIDIA

The scenes in the lunettes of the cross-arms show two stags drinking at the fountain of life. The small pieces of glass or stone used sometimes reflect and sometimes absorb the light, thus giving a realistic depiction of the subjects. The depth of the figures is intensified by the dark blue background and the more vaguely depicted acanthus tendrils. The diffuse light introduced by the translucent alabaster window softens the contours. The frame is typically Greek in origin.

*STAGS AT THE FOUNTAIN OF LIFE* (DETAIL, CROSS-ARMS). *The curved line on the right side of the stag was repeated here to make a symmetrical picture. The cross-stitch technique is not suitable for a circular border.*

# Garland with Fret

SO-CALLED MAUSOLEUM OF GALLA PLACIDIA

The chapel was originally dedicated to St. Lawrence, and for this reason the martyr occupies a place of honor in this chapel. Eager to give up his life, he hurries toward the flames, carrying a cross. An open bookcase contains the four Gospels, for which the martyr will suffer.

*GARLAND WITH FRET* (DETAIL, ARCH OF THE FRONT APSE). *The arch in front of the scene with St. Lawrence is decorated with a colorful border. The use of four times two shades for the recurring geometric motif gives this border a surprising depth.*

# Decorative Borders

CHURCH OF SAN VITALE
BAPTISTERY OF THE CATHEDRAL

The construction of the church was started by Bishop Ecclesius in 525. After his death Bishop Maximian completed and consecrated the church in 548. The brick building in Byzantine style is octagonal in form and has a projecting apse and outrising dome. The many arched windows have translucent alabaster panes.

*DECORATIVE BORDERS*
(DETAILS, SAN VITALE; BAPTISTERY OF THE CATHEDRAL). *All the vaults and arches are covered with mosaics, which means that a wealth of garlands, borders, and frames are found in addition to scenic representations. The basic motif is often the Greek fret decorated with flowers, stars, and precious stones. The borders shown here were taken from one of the arches, from the frame of the scene with Justinian, and also from the vault in the Baptistery of the Cathedral (see page 26).*

# Peacock with Flowers

CHURCH OF SAN VITALE

The interior of San Vitale is of impressive beauty. Eight piers extend upward to the *matronem* (women's gallery) and form a solid support for the dome. The arches, as well as the walls and the vault in the apse, are decorated with mosaics. The most remarkable are those depicting Emperor Justinian on one side and his wife Theodora on the opposite wall, offering imperial gifts. The San Vitale mosaics show for the first time the changed conception of the relationship between ecclesiastical and temporal power.

*PEACOCK WITH FLOWERS* (DETAIL, APSE). *The semi-dome of the apse shows Christ surrounded by archangels, San Vitale, and Bishop Ecclesius. The Kingdom of Heaven, in which they are shown, is symbolized by birds and flowers.*

# Peter and Andrew Follow Jesus

BASILICA OF SANT' APOLLINARE NUOVO

In the early sixth century Theodoric's palace-church was called San Martino in Ciel d'Oro. After the relics of St. Apollinaris were brought to Ravenna its name was altered. The church is built in typical Ravenna style. The tall, round belfry has mullioned windows which gradually increase in size in the upper stories. A marble porch was erected in the sixteenth century.

*PETER AND ANDREW FOLLOW JESUS* (DETAIL, LEFT WALL). *The scene shown is found in the top strip of the left wall. It is a refined mosaic, showing even the fish in the net.*

# The Royal Palace of Theodoric

BASILICA OF SANT' APOLLINARE NUOVO

Soil subsidence made restoration of the basilica necessary in the sixteenth century. The raising of the twenty-four columns altered the distance between the arches and the mosaics, making the proportions different from the architect's intention. The mosaics on the right and left walls are not by the same artist. Those on the left are more refined, although both artists were inspired by contemporary miniatures from Constantinople. At the top of the walls are panels depicting scenes from the life of Christ. The middle strip has alternating arched windows and mosaic representations of prophets. The bottom strip on the right wall shows twenty-six martyrs leaving Theodoric's palace, bearing crowns, and proceeding slowly toward the Redeemer.

THE ROYAL PALACE OF THEODORIC (DETAIL, RIGHT WALL, BOTTOM STRIP). *The figures originally depicted in the palace were effaced and replaced by white hangings. The hands of a few remain halfway down the columns, and the outline of their heads may still be seen. In the model shown these details were left out.*

# Adoration of the Magi
BASILICA OF SANT' APOLLINARE NUOVO

The left part of the church was reserved for women. On this wall the large strip shows twenty-two saints, clothed in white and golden robes. They are leaving the harbor of Classe to follow the three Magi, bearing gifts for the Virgin and Child.

*ADORATION OF THE MAGI* (DETAIL, LEFT WALL, BOTTOM STRIP). *The Magi are represented in motion, thus providing a contrast with the static procession of the saints. Their gorgeous eastern clothes, as well as the expression in their faces, make them real individuals: Melchior, Balthasar, and Caspar.*

# Garland and Decorative Borders

BAPTISTERY OF THE CATHEDRAL

Although their dating is still contested, it seems that the Baptistery mosaics date from the episcopacy of Bishop Neon, 450 A.D. The baptistery is octagonal in plan with three projecting apses and is covered with a dome. The mosaics on the spandrels and arches of the lower zone consist of a blue background with green and golden acanthus tendrils.

In the upper zone, the windows are flanked by arches decorated with golden leaf-motifs on a red or blue background. The hanging dome is covered with mosaics. The main motif is the Baptism of Christ. The sanctity of the Gospels (open book) and the omnipotence of the Holy Trinity (empty chairs) are symbolized in the drum of the dome. The realistic representation of the figures in the dome prove the distance of the artists from the Byzantine tradition.

GARLAND AND DECORATIVE BORDERS (DETAIL, VAULT; DETAIL, MAUSOLEUM OF GALLA PLACIDIA). *The borders shown here come from arch decorations in the mausoleum of Galla Placidia (see page 10).*
*They frame a detail from the lower band of decoration in the vault of the baptistery.*

# Ornament with Birds

BASILICA OF SANT' APOLLINARE IN CLASSE

This imposing basilica was built in 534 beside the tomb of St. Apollinaris, the first martyr of Ravenna. In those days Classe was an important harbor. Due to disafflorestation, the harbor silted up and was abandoned. The basilica remained standing in its present lonely situation. Inside the church twelve arches are supported by marble columns on either side of the nave. At the center of the apse vault St. Apollinaris stands in green paradise-like scenery, surrounded by sheep, flowers, and birds. Above his head is a great cross among myriads of stars. On either side are Elijah and Moses.

*ORNAMENT WITH BIRDS* (DETAIL, VAULT). *The motif shown is found in the outer circle of the vault. The borders on both sides of the ornament frame the triumphal arch.*

# Design of Flowers and Fowl

ARCHIESPISCOPAL CHAPEL

The chapel, dedicated to St. Andrew, was erected by Peter II at the end of the fourth century. It was the the private chapel of the bishops of Ravenna.

The square chapel is in the form of a Greek cross with four piers forming arches and supporting a groined vault.

All the vaults are covered with mosaics. Medallions representing Christ, the twelve Apostles, and twelve saints are set on a golden background. Many of the mosaics have been restored and their quality affected. Best conserved are the mosaics in the vestibule. Above the door stands the figure of the Militant Christ, conquering lion and snake, carrying the Cross. An open book in His left hand reads: "I am the Way, the Truth, and the Life."

*DESIGN OF FLOWERS AND FOWL* (VAULT, VESTIBULE).
*On a golden background a refined design consisting of lilies, stylized roses, and various birds covers the vault in the vestibule. The picture shows this motif with a border which is not found in the original mosaic.*

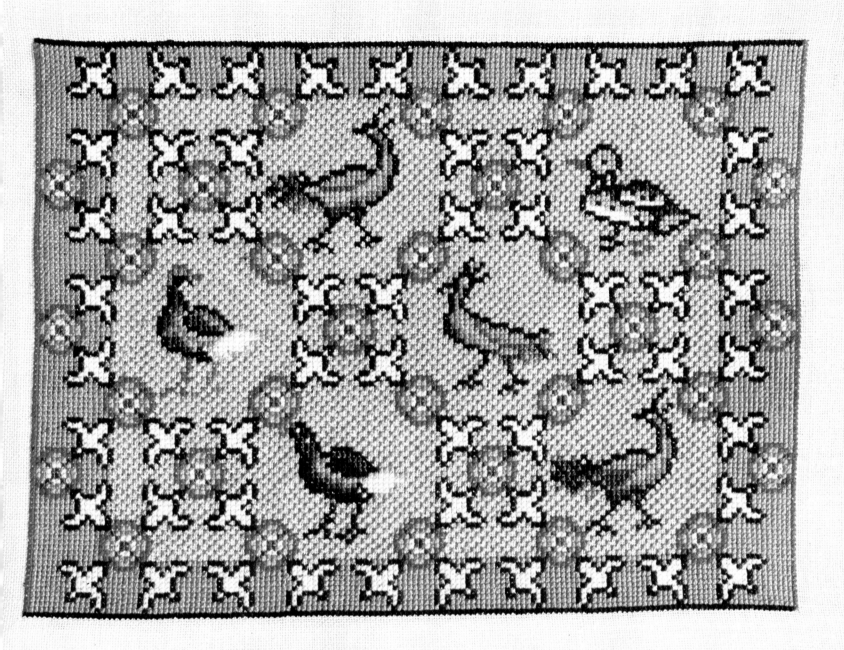

# Sample Interior

1 TABLECLOTH. The Greek border with flowers on page 17 is used here as a closed border. It is made from evenweave fabric with 18 threads per square inch, using whole threads of DMC embroidery silk.

2, 3 COFFEE-COSY AND WASTE-PAPER BASKET. Both are made from tapestry canvas using whole threads of DMC embroidery silk. The coffee-cosy is based on the design shown on page 13. The motif was embroidered twice and then joined to a strip embroidered with the bottom border. The motif on page 19 was used for the waste-paper basket. Embroidered twice, it covers an empty detergent barrel, lined inside with contact paper.

4, 5 RUG AND CUSHION. Both are made in smyrna technique, using sudan wool and sudan canvas. For the rug the motif on page 31 was used. The cushion shows a detail from the design on page 11 on a white background.

6 KELIM CUSHION, based on the design on page 27. Tapestry wool and tapestry canvas were used. The border was embroidered on four sides, making it possible to form a vertical strip.

7 FRAMED PICTURE, based on the design on page 15. Half crosses were made alternately from top to bottom and vice-versa, thus forming small Vs. Tapestry canvas and whole threads of DMC embroidery silk were used.

8 MOSAIC TILE, based on detail from the design on page 31.

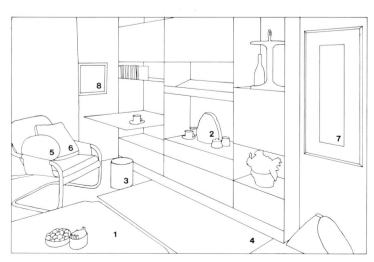

32

# General Instructions

The color plates on pages 11, 13, 15, 17, 23, 27, and 29 show the embroideries in their original sizes, while those on pages 9, 19, 21, 25, and 31 were reduced by 15%. The needlework is mainly cross-stitch and only occasionally is straight stitch used to accentuate the outlines. Fine evenweave fabric with 30 threads per inch was used for the models.

Color indications for each design are given according to the color chart of DMC embroidery silk. On this fine fabric two strands of silk were used. Where only one strand was used, it is indicated beside the number with a ',e.g., 734'.

To avoid confusing the shades it may be helpful to glue a thread of the appropriate color on the number of the embroidery silk.

The samples on pages 32 and 33 show the use of these designs in varying techniques. In all these cases the patterns given in this book can be used.

If executed with other materials, the colors will differ more or less from the originals. The color chart on page 35 can be useful in matching the right colors.

The motifs on pages 11, 15, 17, 27, 29, and 31 can be repeated as often as necessary, and all color variations are possible. The garland with fret on page 15 needs four times two shades, thus giving a three-dimensional quality to the motif. All corners can be found on the patterns, making it possible to embroider closed borders.

The use of different materials will be discussed under techniques.

The patterns for the embroideries appear on pages 40–63, in the same sequence as the color plates.

# Color Chart

These numbers refer to DMC embroidery silk.

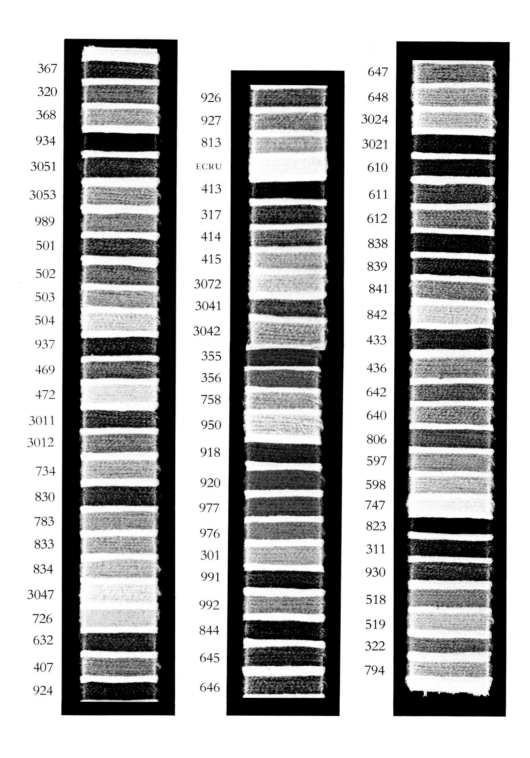

| | | |
|---|---|---|
| 367 | 926 | 647 |
| 320 | 927 | 648 |
| 368 | 813 | 3024 |
| 934 | ECRU | 3021 |
| 3051 | 413 | 610 |
| 3053 | 317 | 611 |
| 989 | 414 | 612 |
| 501 | 415 | 838 |
| 502 | 3072 | 839 |
| 503 | 3041 | 841 |
| 504 | 3042 | 842 |
| 937 | 355 | 433 |
| 469 | 356 | 436 |
| 472 | 758 | 642 |
| 3011 | 950 | 640 |
| 3012 | 918 | 806 |
| 734 | 920 | 597 |
| 830 | 977 | 598 |
| 783 | 976 | 747 |
| 833 | 301 | 823 |
| 834 | 991 | 311 |
| 3047 | 992 | 930 |
| 726 | 844 | 518 |
| 632 | 645 | 519 |
| 407 | 646 | 322 |
| 924 | | 794 |

# Smyrna Technique

Several motifs in this book are suitable for the smyrna technique. Smyrna wool and smyrna canvas are the best materials for making rugs and carpets. Sudan materials are more advisable for smaller objects since dimensions would become too large if smyrna materials were used.

Two methods can be followed in the smyrna technique. The first method uses a needle and a small lath. A long thread is worked around the lath, row by row. The nooses of several rows are cut together. The second method uses cut threads. The length of the threads depends on the desired pile and on the thickness of the wool. To cut the wool, special laths are available in needlework shops. Cutting can be done easily, using a Stanley knife. A so-called smyrna needle (a special crochet needle) is used to make the knots, one by one, as shown in the illustration.

For the patterns in this book, since many colors have been used, the second method is best. Each square of the pattern represents one knot. The background must always be filled in with a neutral color. The sides can be given a finishing touch by making a braided border. The canvas is folded back two holes outside the knotting work. A long woollen thread the color of the outside border is used to make long stitches around the canvas, taking four holes to the right, three holes to the left, working back and forth. The needle is always placed at the backside of the canvas. At the corners several stitches are made in the same hole, to cover the canvas completely. This border is very beautiful for cushions as well as rugs. The size, if smyrna wool and smyrna canvas are used, will be four times the size of the original; if sudan materials are used the size will be three and one half times that of the original.

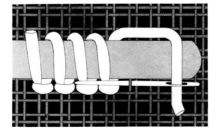 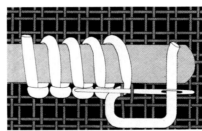

 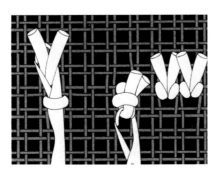

# Kelim Technique

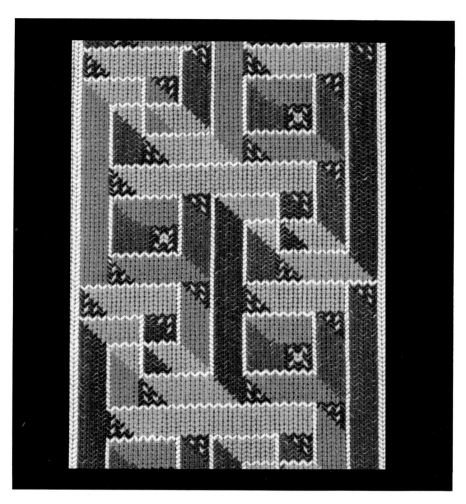

This technique is suitable for cushions, runners, and small rugs. Sudan wool and sudan canvas suit this technique best although small objects such as cushions can be made with tapestry wool and tapestry canvas.

The stitch has a V-form, like a mesh-stitch. The work must be done in rows, working half the V from top to bottom, the other half next to it from bottom to top. Each square in the pattern represents half the V. In the vertical direction the stitches pass two threads of the canvas, as shown in the illustration. It is preferable to work either with more than one color at the same time, or to do the outlines first, to avoid errors in working in the right direction.
The background must always be filled in with a neutral color. The size, if worked with the sudan material, will be three and one half times the size of the original; if tapestry wool and tapestry canvas are used the size will be one and one half times that of the original.

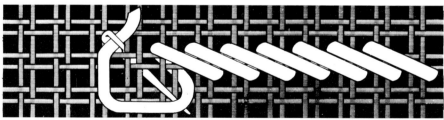

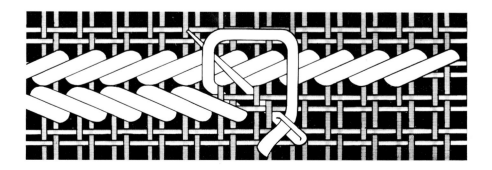

# Cross-Stitch Technique

Cross-stitch is one of the oldest and most popular techniques. The choice of the material is very important. Every even-weave fabric which has the same number of threads per inch in each direction of the fabric is suitable. The use of DMC embroidery silk is preferable, as the number of used strands can be adapted to the coarseness of the fabric. Moreover, this material has the greatest number of colors available.

The best results are obtained if worked as much as possible from bottom up, thus forming a half cross up to the end of the row, completing the other half as shown. Start, as a rule, at the center of the pattern, marking the center of the fabric with a thread. It is also preferable to start with the darkest colors. The use of straight stitches is indicated on the pattern. The lines used are shown on the color key. Straight stitches must always be made after finishing the cross-stitches.

If certain objects need other than evenweave fabric, the following method can be used: A special embroidery canvas is basted on the desired fabric, both materials laying flat. The position of the design is marked with a thread. The needle should be drawn vertically and both layers taken together. Special care should be taken to draw the needle through the holes of the canvas and not catch the warp or weft. The thread should be drawn tightly. When the cross-stitch embroidery is finished, the threads of the canvas are drawn out one by one. The embroidery will remain on the second fabric. Only at this point should straight stitches be made.

Apart from the materials mentioned above, tapestry wool and canvas can be used. In this case only half crosses are made on the canvas. This technique is very suitable for cushions, chairs, etc. The background must always be filled in with a suitable neutral color. The size will be one and one half times that of the original.

# Mosaic Technique

The sample in this book was made with Talens mosaic stones, measuring 2/5 square inch. Since few colors are available, the result will differ considerably from the originals. Nevertheless, starting with the basic colors red, green, blue, etc., good results can be obtained. A mixture of bright colors will make the background look more natural.

The stones must be glued row by row according to the pattern. Use a good hobby adhesive. The underlayer can be cardboard, glass, or wood. If a nice underlayer is used, glueing just the motif will be sufficient; on other materials the background must be filled in with neutral bright colors. The size will be six times that of the original.

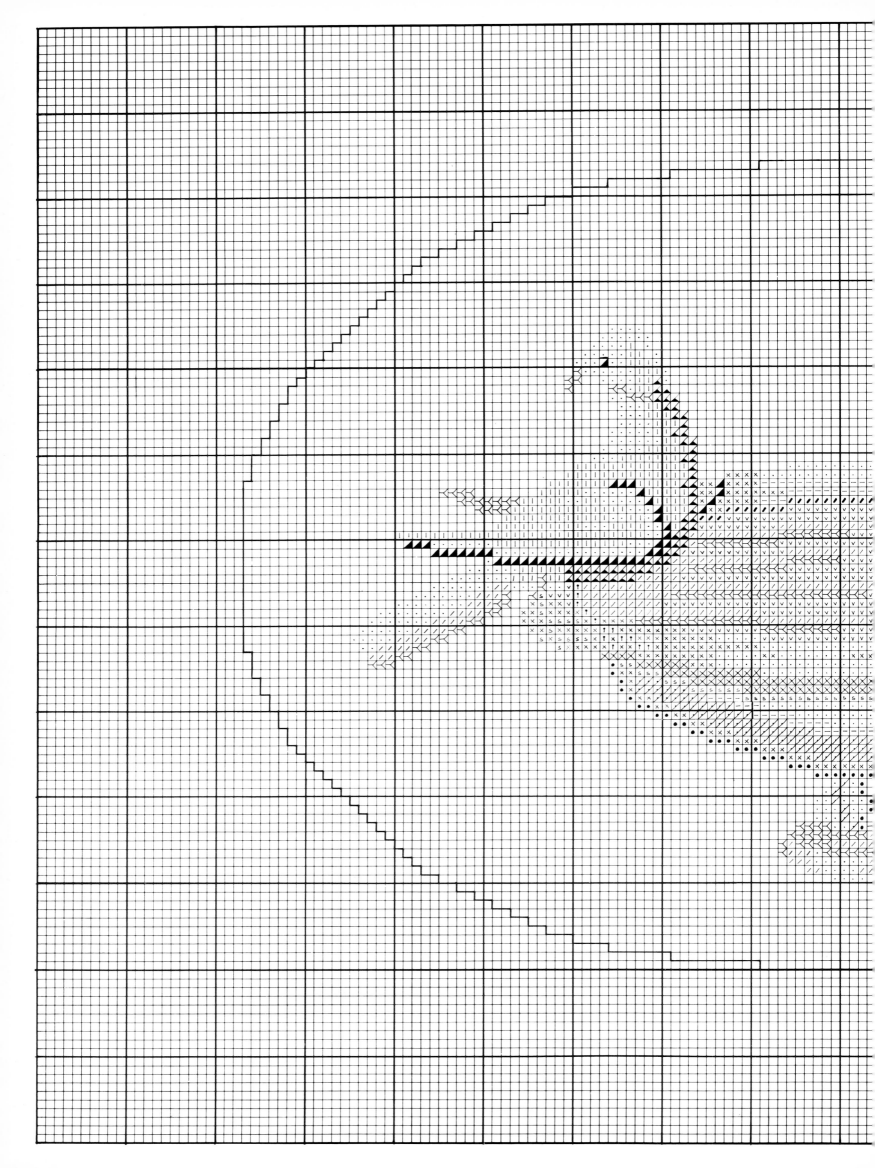

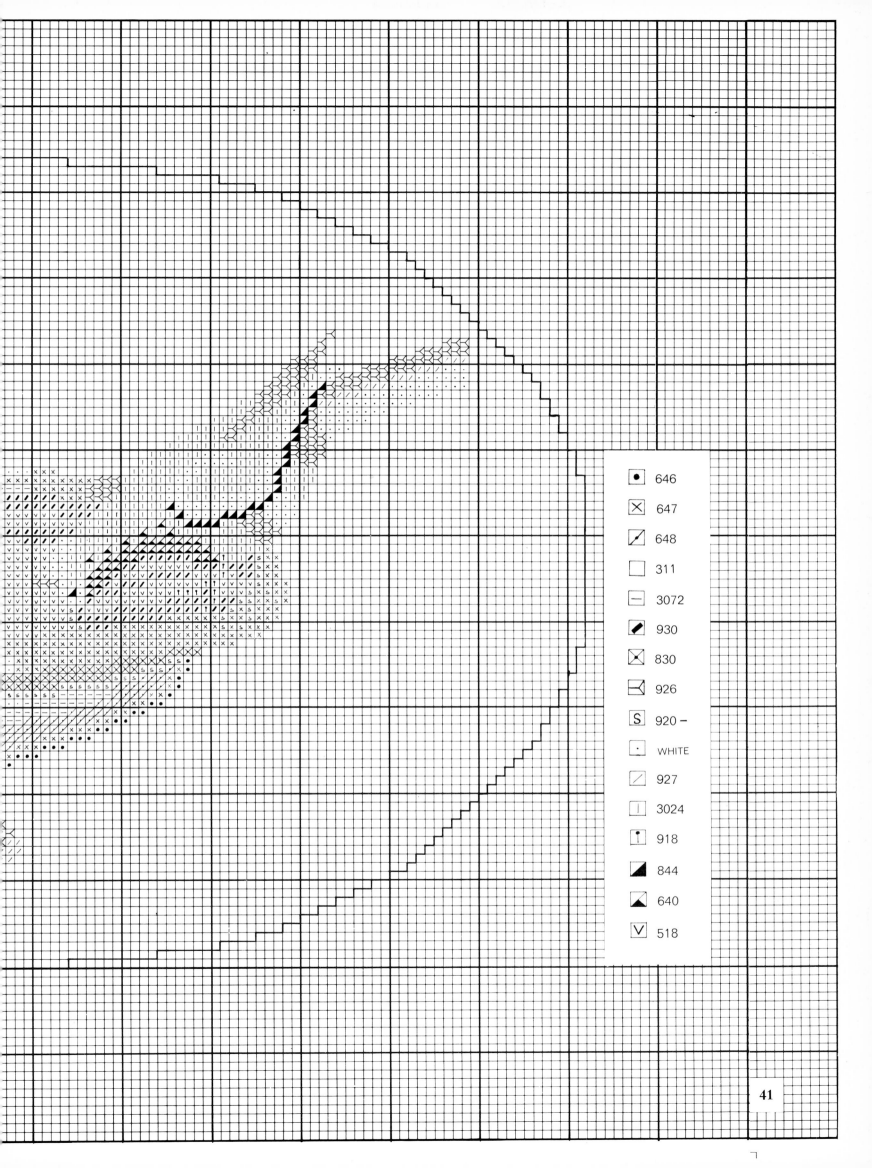

| | |
|---|---|
| • | 646 |
| ✕ | 647 |
| ⁄ | 648 |
| ☐ | 311 |
| — | 3072 |
| ◢ | 930 |
| ⊠ | 830 |
| ◺ | 926 |
| S | 920 – |
| · | WHITE |
| ⁄ | 927 |
| ⊓ | 3024 |
| ↑ | 918 |
| ◣ | 844 |
| ◤ | 640 |
| V | 518 |

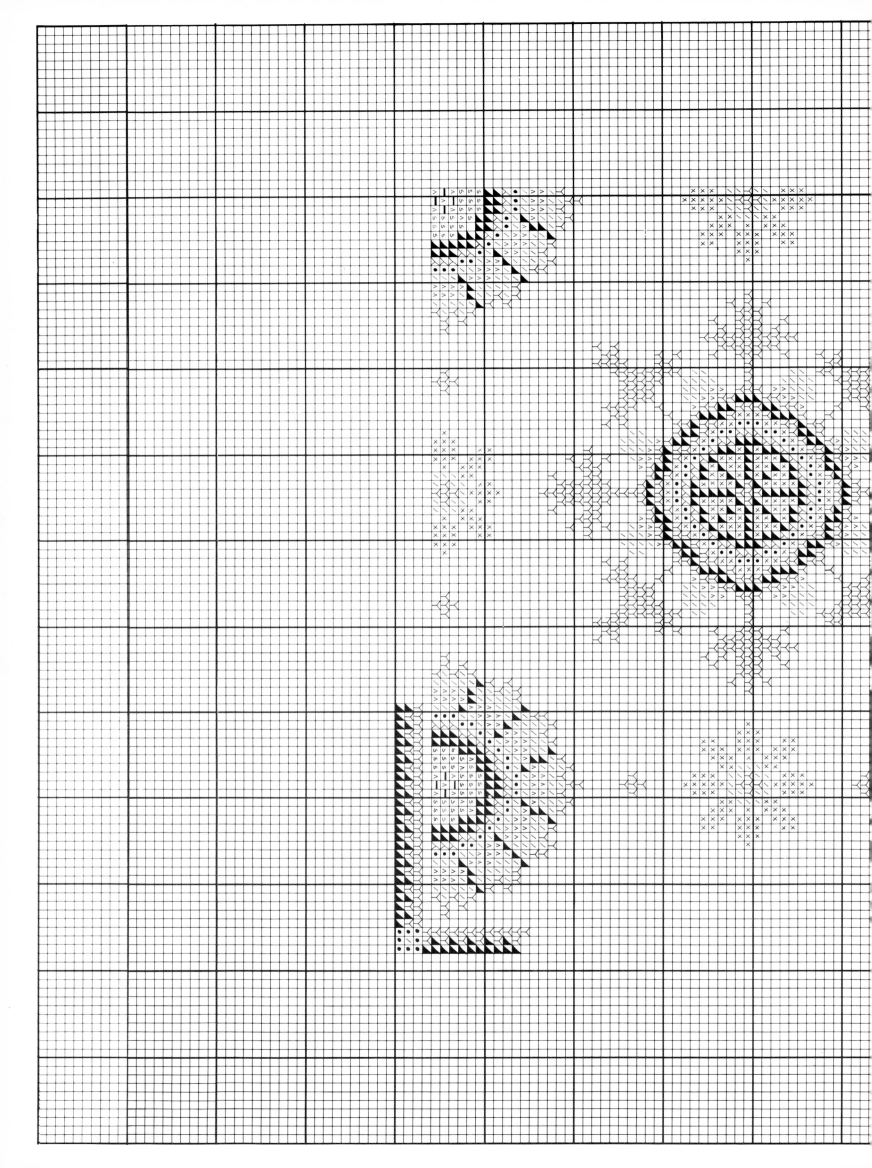

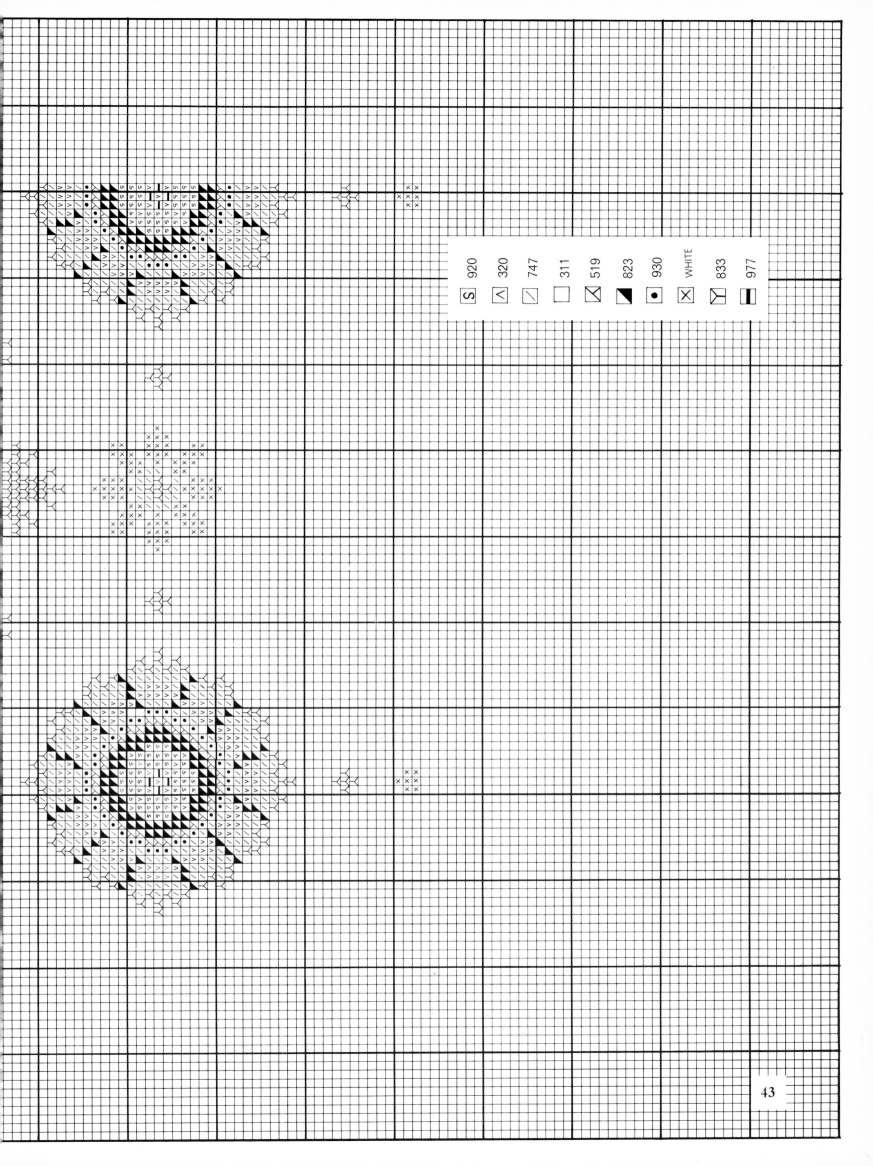

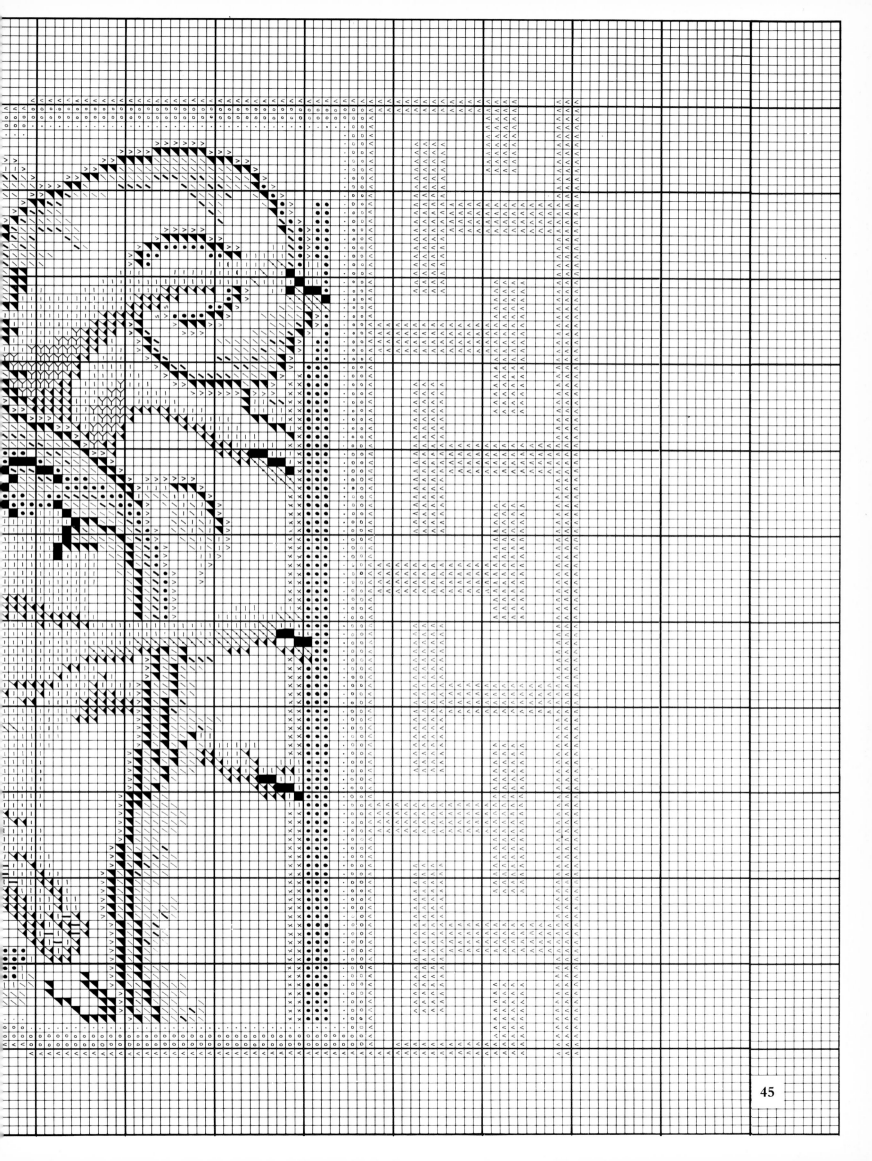

45

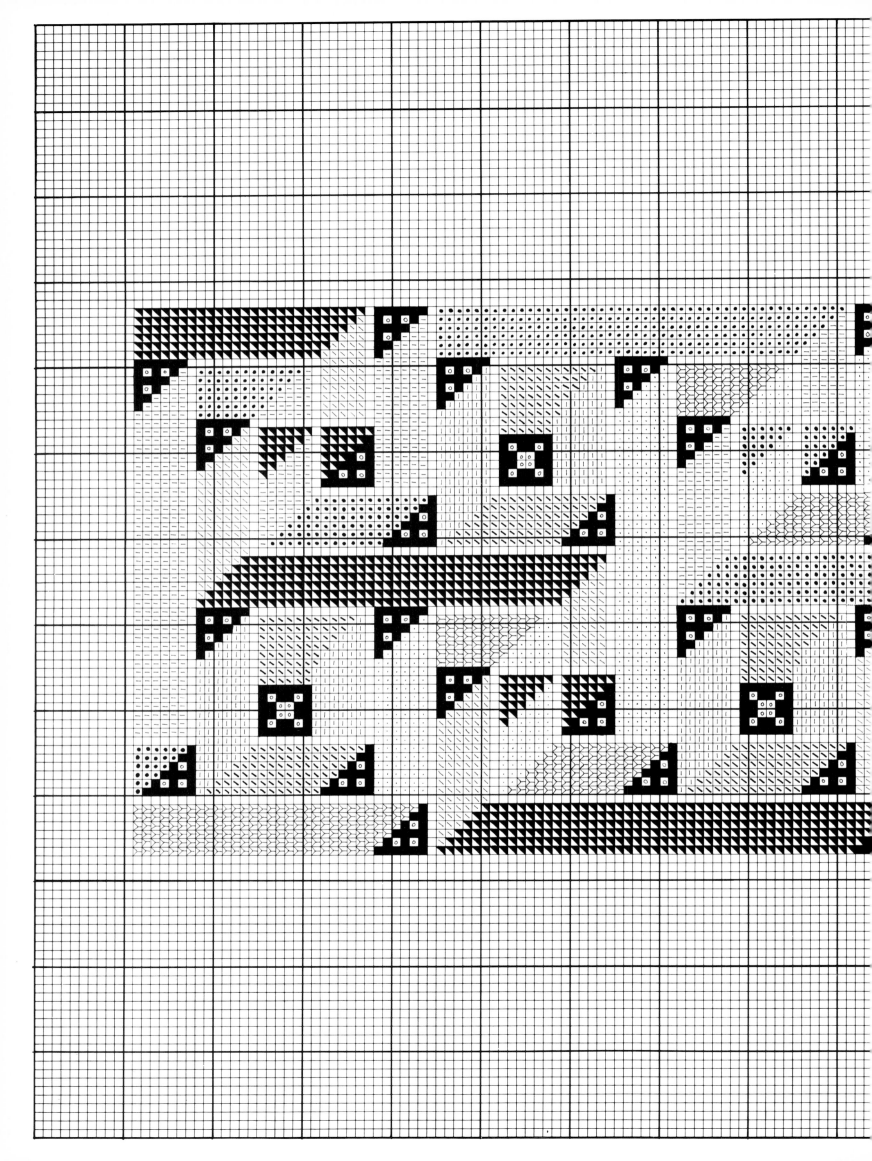

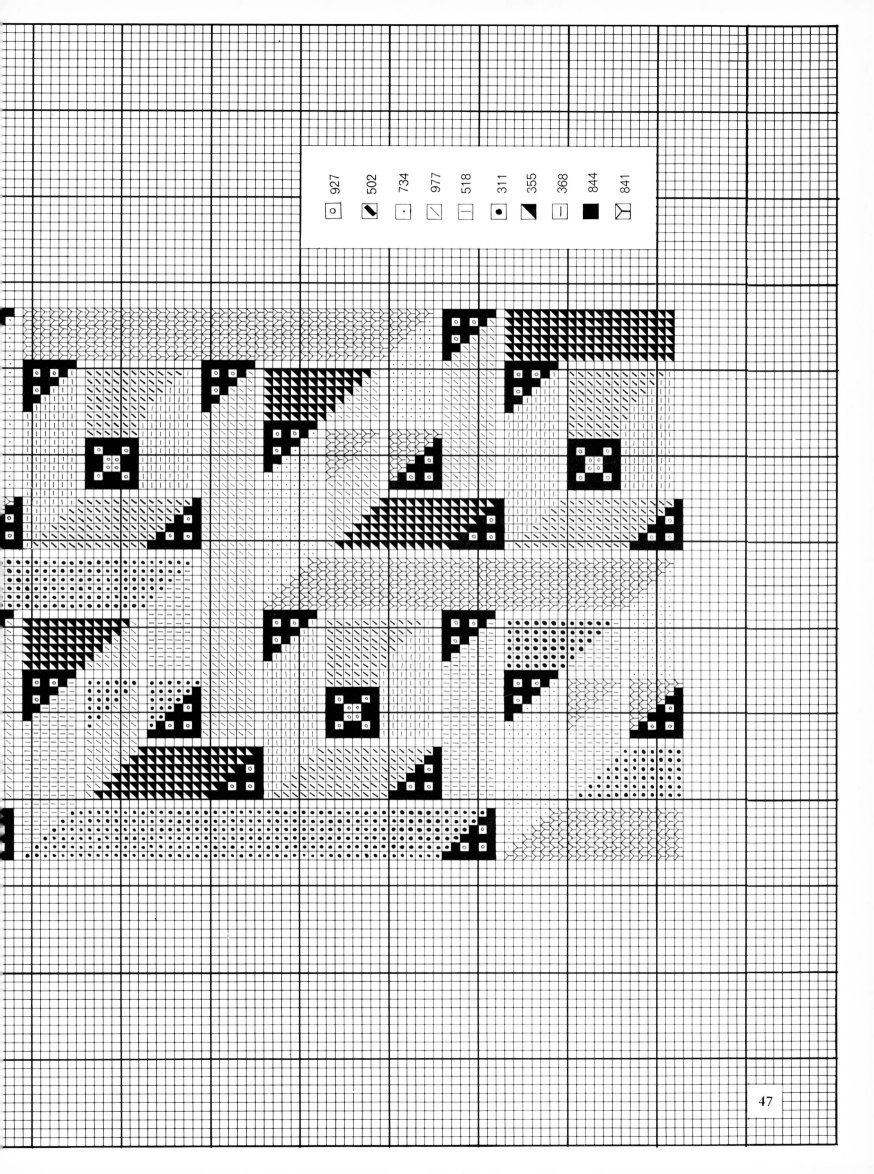

47

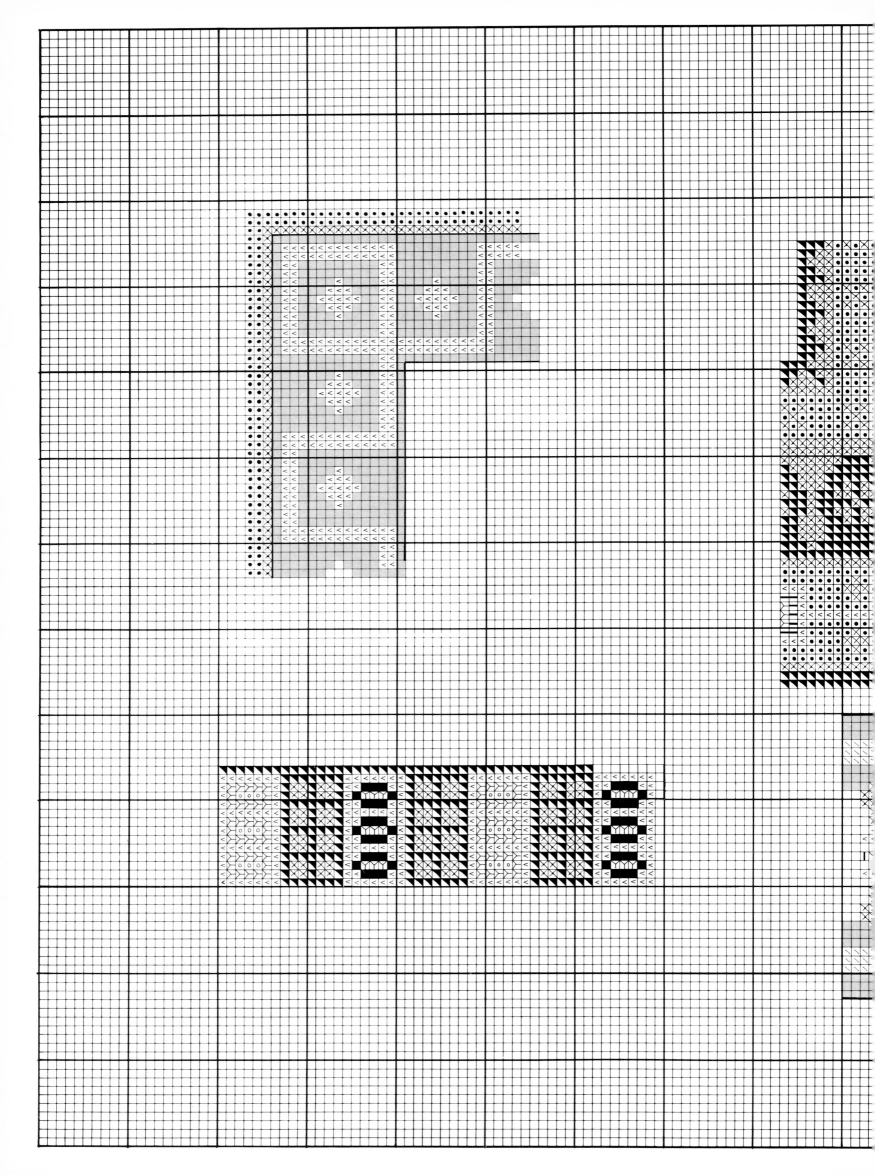

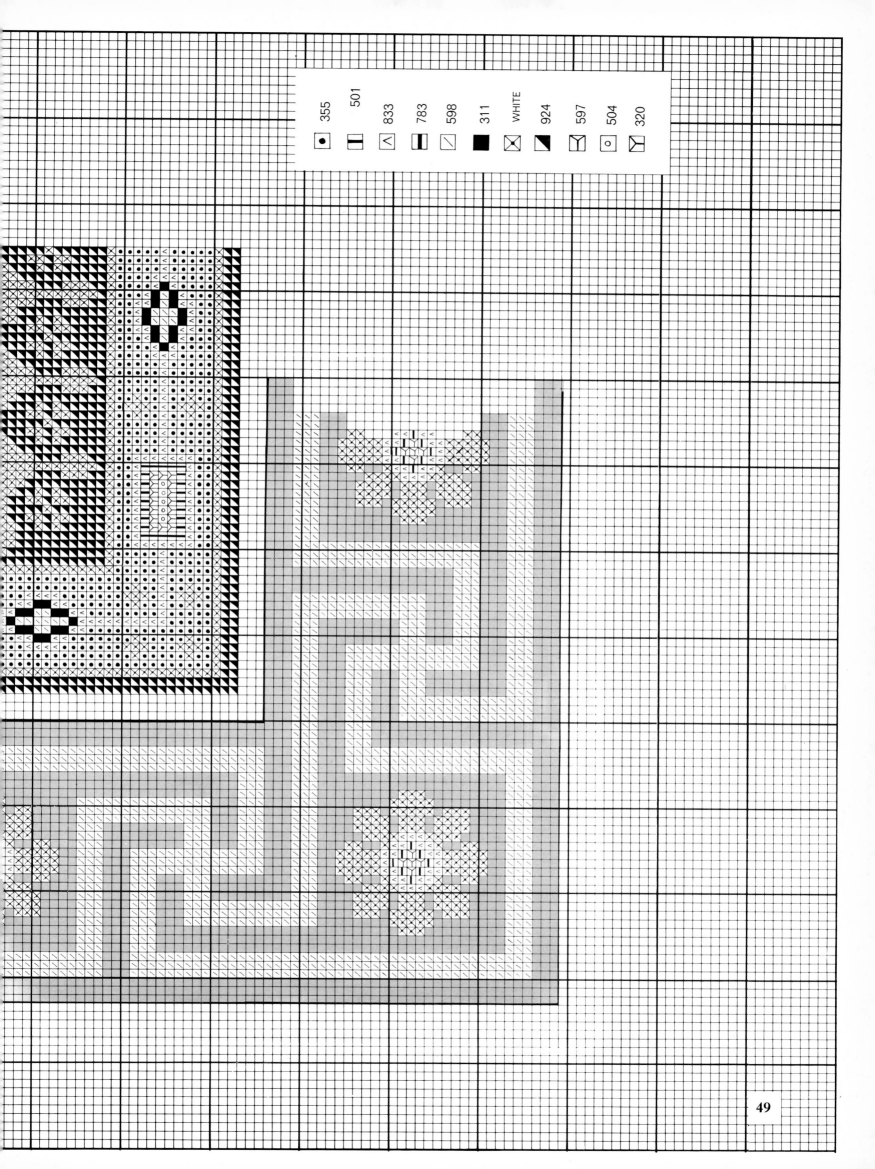

| | |
|---|---|
| ⊡ | 930 |
| ⊠ | 367 |
| ⧄ | 833 |
| ▭ | 647 |
| ▭ | 924' |
| ■ | 844 |
| ⊠ | 3012 |
| ⊙ | 813 |
| ▢ | 734' |
| ◥ | 501' |
| ▯ | 3051 |
| ⋀ | 368 |
| ⊢ | 414 |
| S | 301 |
| ⋅ | WHITE |
| ⧄ | 320' |
| ⏐ | 503' |
| ◩ | 926 |
| ◣ | 823 |
| ◥ | 355 |
| V | 927 |
| Y | 322 |

51

| | | | |
|---|---|---|---|
| L | 317 | ● | 632 |
| ⊢ | 842 | ✕ | 841 |
| S | 355 | ╱ | 647 |
| · | WHITE | ▬ | 930 |
| ╱ | 927 | − | 950 |
| ▯ | 758 | ■ | 823 |
| ◣ | 844 | ⊠ | 991 |
| ◢ | 413 | ⊡ | 597 |
| ◤ | 311 | ⫯ | 977 |
| V | 318 | ╲ | 747 |
| Y | 3041 | ▮ | 839 |
| ◹ | 3024 | + | 834 |
| ○ | 726 | ⊡ | 734 |
| /N | 937 | ⫼ | 469 |
| ◥ | 3012 | ╲ | 598 |
| ▲ | 646 | ⫯ | 3042 |
| ∧ | 612 | ◢ | 3011 |
| ⌐ | ,794 | ◣ | 806 |

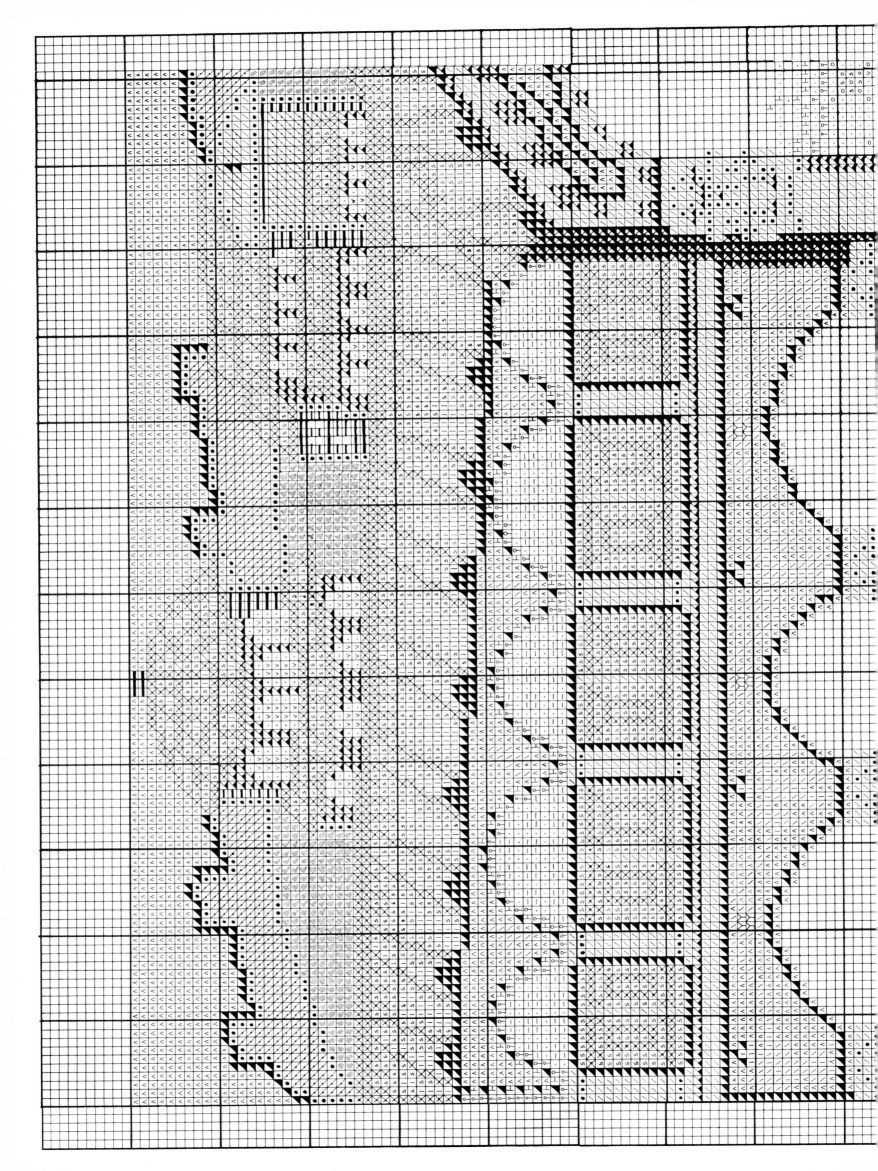

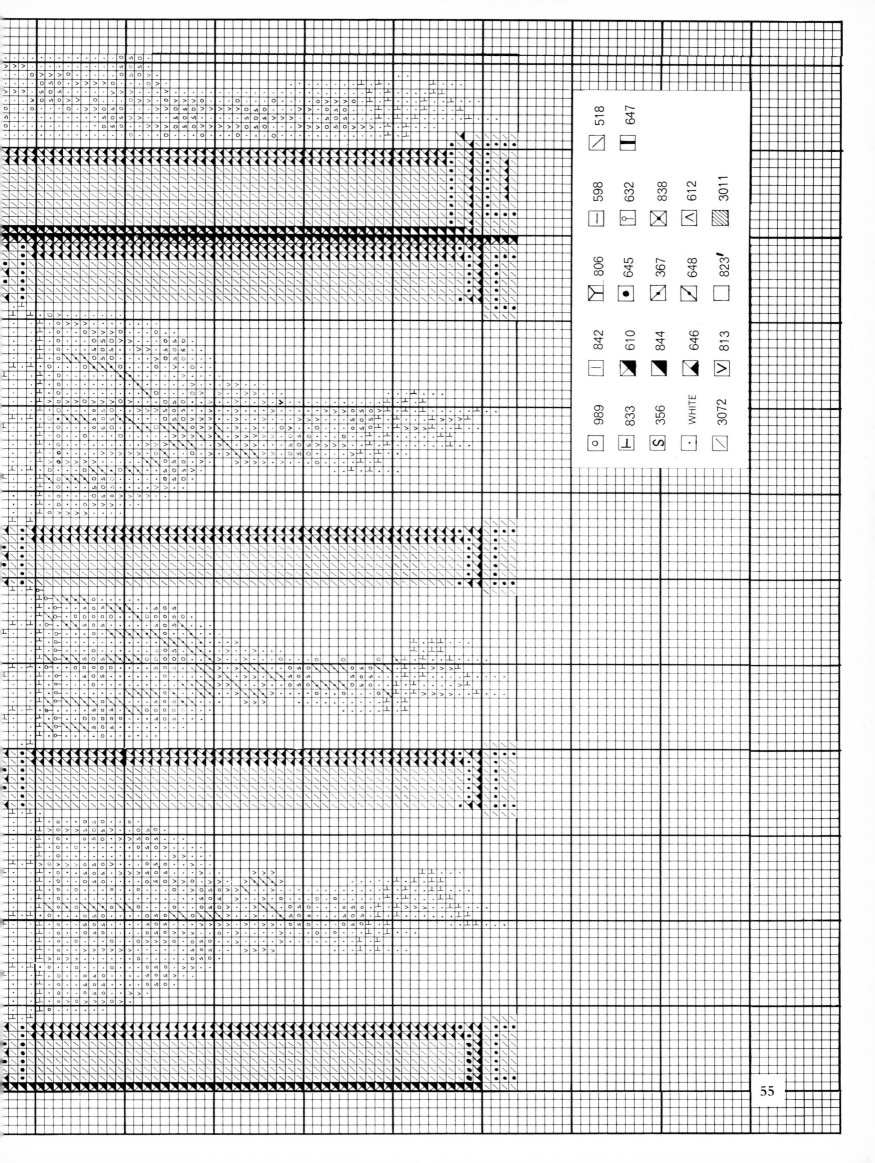

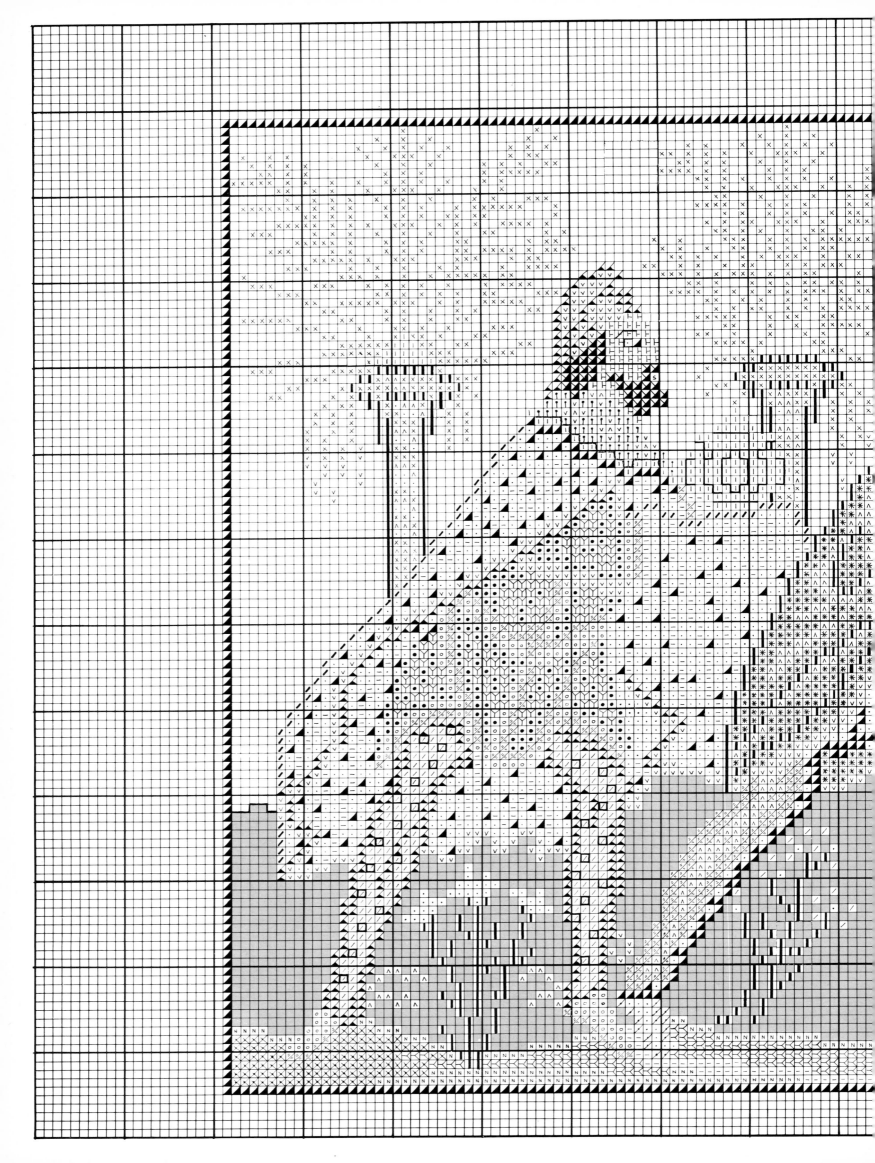

| Symbol | Color |
|--------|-------|
| ◢ | 311 |
| ◺ | 926 |
| ● | 413 |
| ✕ | 367 |
| ◿ | 318 |
| ⊸ | 828 |
| — | 927 |
| ⌐ | 317 |
| ⊠ | 924 |
| ▢ | 611′ |
| ⌶ | 519 |
| ◥ | 415 |
| ⊢ | 842 |
| S | 355 |
| ∴ | WHITE |
| ╱ | 977 |
| ‖ | 3072 |
| ◣ | 838 |
| ◣ | 844 — |
| ◀ | 918 — |
| V | 976 |
| Y | 3042 |
| ▮ | 934 |
| ∧ | 834 |
| ▨ | 830 |
| ╱ | 930 |
| ✳ | 320 |
| N | 937 |
| ◦ | 3047 |
| ▨ | 320′ |

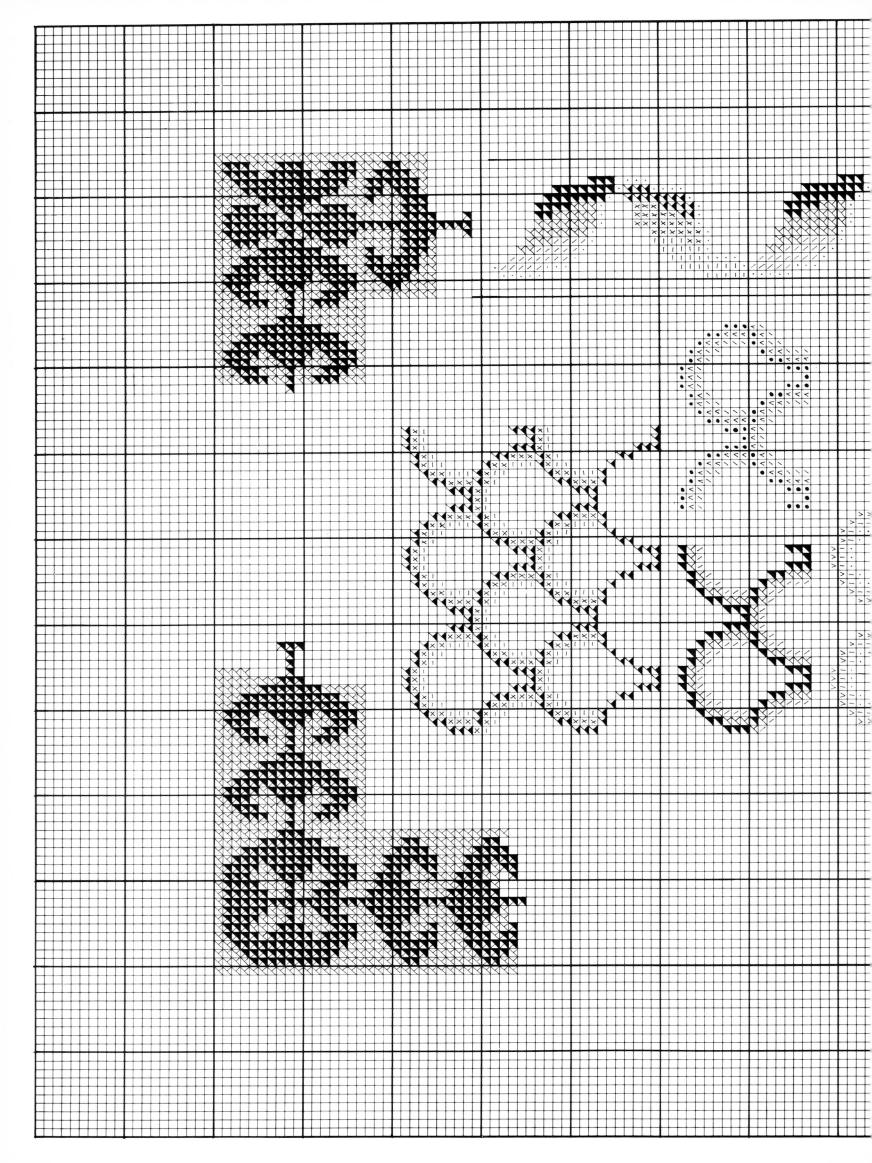

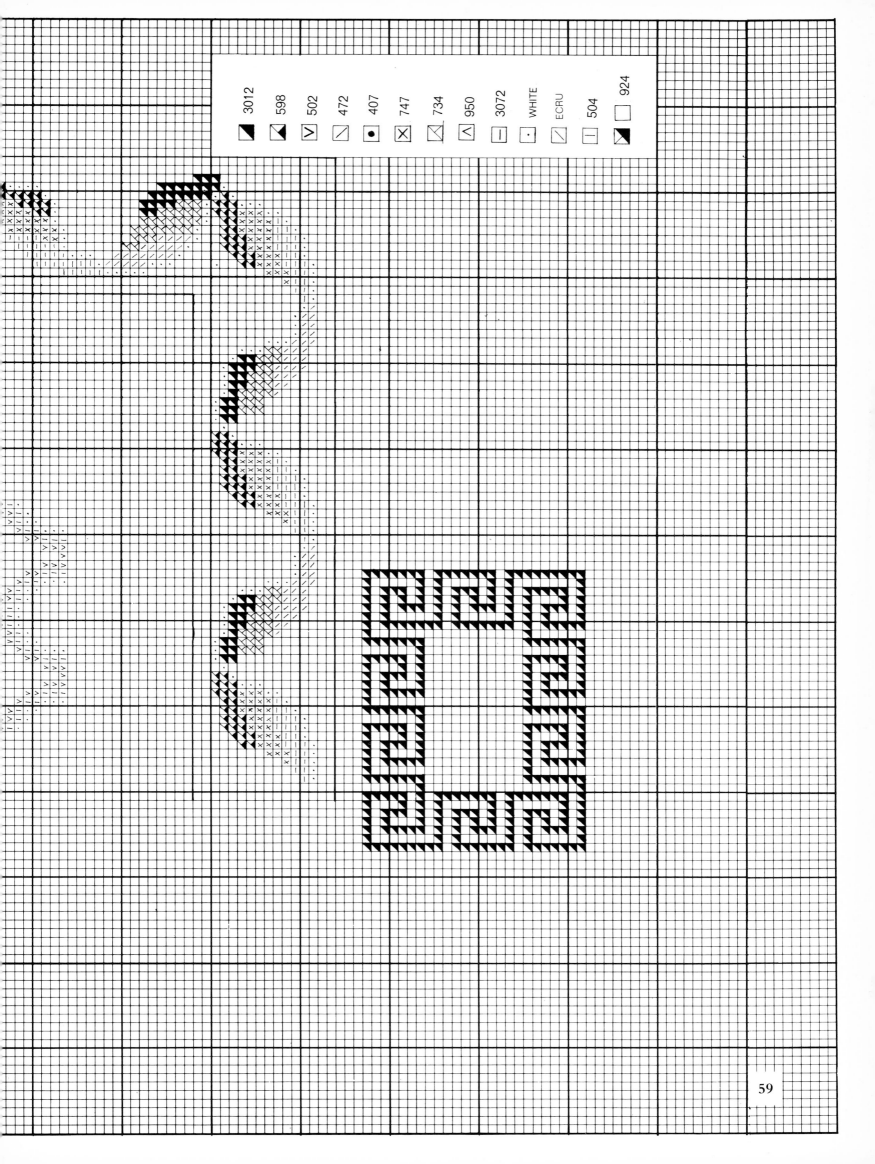

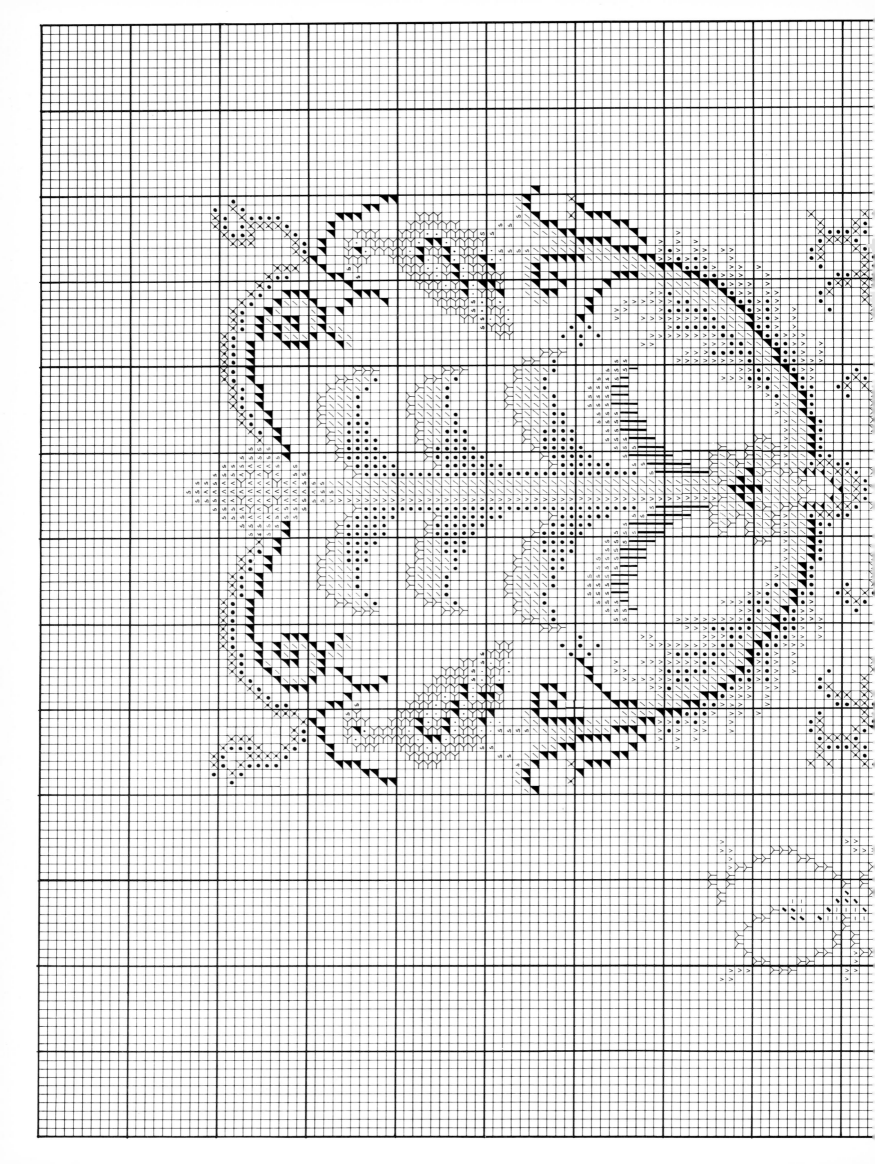

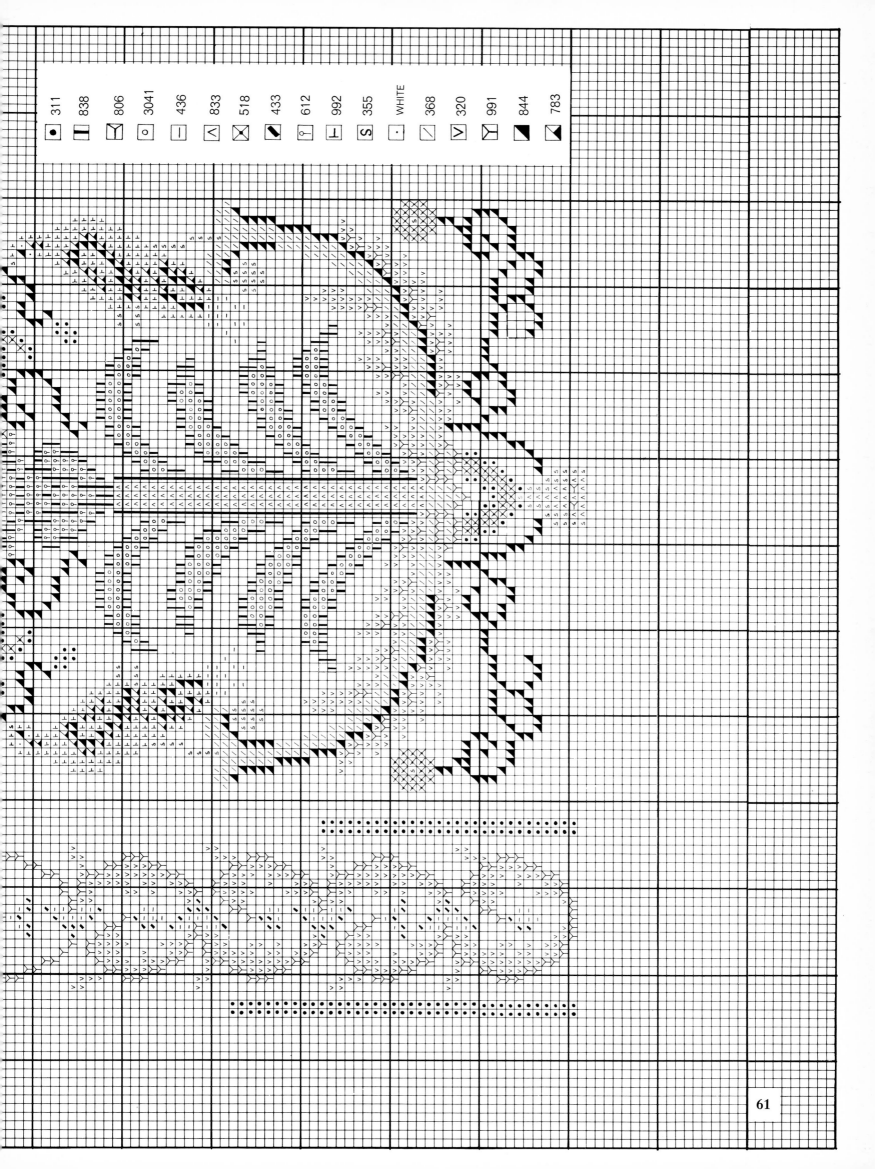

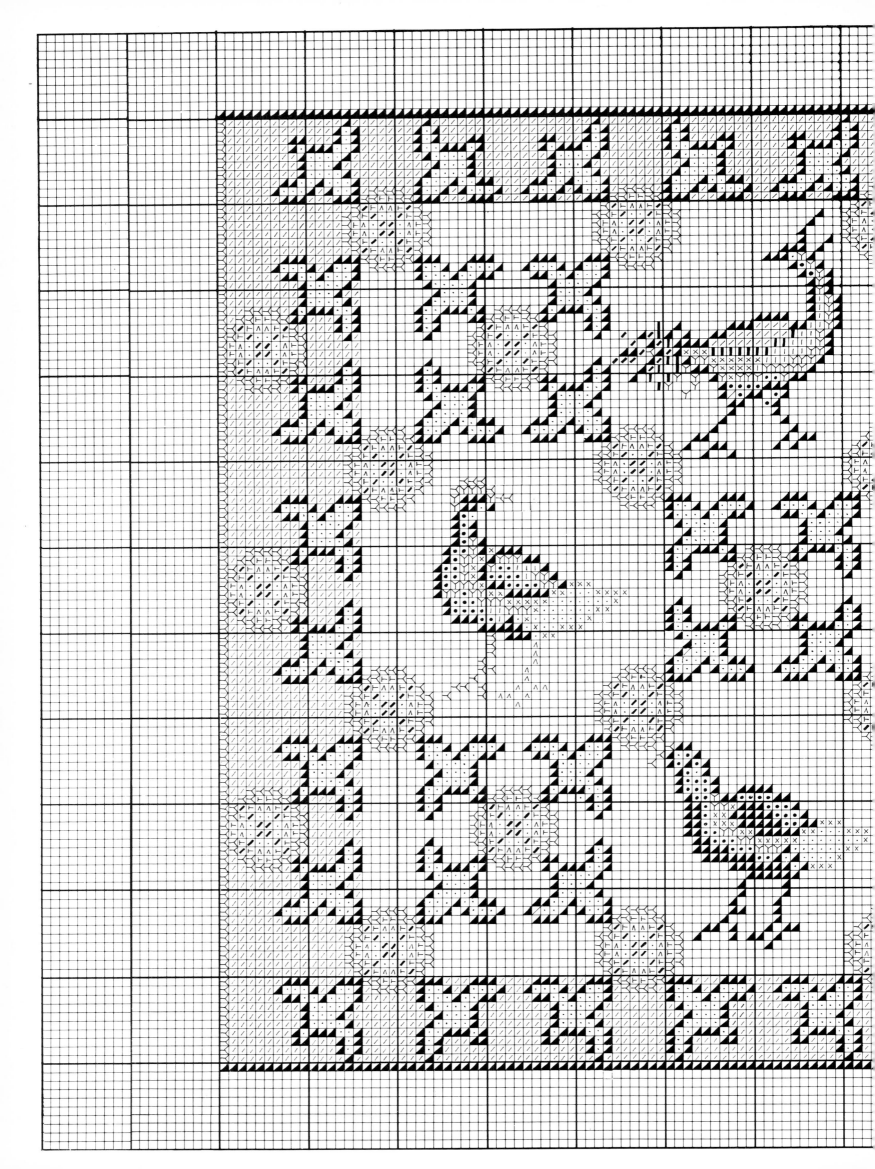

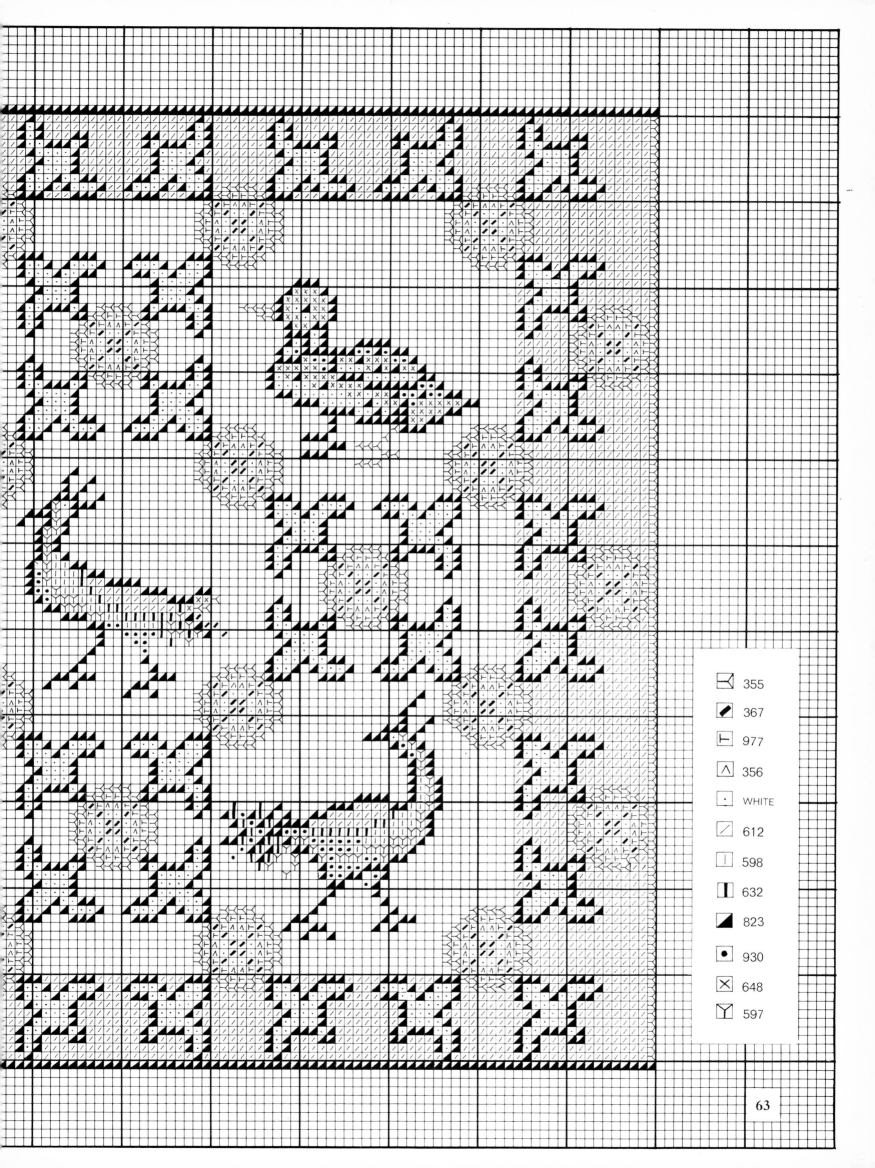

| | |
|---|---|
| ◹ | 355 |
| ◨ | 367 |
| ⊢ | 977 |
| ∧ | 356 |
| · | WHITE |
| ╱ | 612 |
| ▯ | 598 |
| ▮ | 632 |
| ◣ | 823 |
| ● | 930 |
| ✕ | 648 |
| ⊻ | 597 |

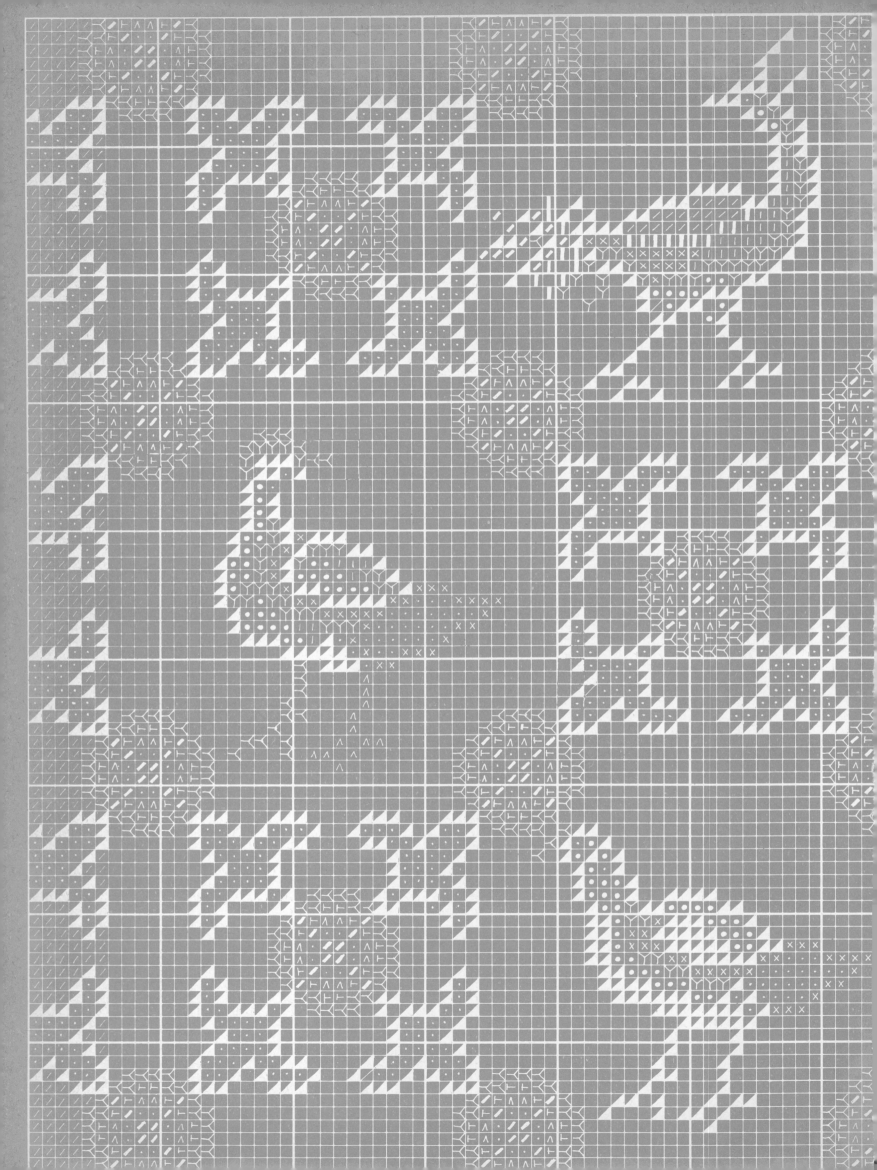